School is Where We All Belong

A Story About Building a Sense of Belonging Outside of Home

Kelly-Ann Allen and Michael Wagner
Illustrated by Kathryn Kallady

 Routledge
Taylor & Francis Group

LONDON AND NEW YORK

Designed cover image: Kathryn Kallady

First published 2025
by Routledge
4 Park Square, Milton Park, Abingdon, Oxon OX14 4RN

and by Routledge
605 Third Avenue, New York, NY 10158

Routledge is an imprint of the Taylor & Francis Group, an informa business

British Library Cataloguing-in-Publication Data
A catalogue record for this book is available from the British Library

ISBN: 978-1-032-46577-7 (pbk)
ISBN: 978-1-003-38237-9 (ebk)

This book can also be purchased as part of a set: *Conceptual Playworlds for Belonging* (set), 978-1-032-46583-8

DOI: 10.4324/9781003382379

Typeset in Minion Pro
by Deanta Global Publishing Services, Chennai, India

For Product Safety Concerns and Information please contact our EU representative GPSR@taylorandfrancis.com Taylor & Francis Verlag GmbH, Kaufingerstraße 24, 80331 München, Germany.
Batch No. NP105634

SCHOOL IS WHERE WE ALL BELONG

School is Where We All Belong is a beautifully illustrated story book that helps to develop a sense of belonging in children, particularly at school. It narrates the different ways by which five characters identify their feelings of belonging to school through the five senses (hearing, touch, smell, taste, and sight).

With its engaging illustrations and narrative, children are encouraged to share their own experiences at the end of each character's story, which allows them to develop a better sense of school belonging, sharing the message that belonging is largely experiential and special to each person.

School belonging is an important ingredient for many positive outcomes for student learning and wellbeing. This story provides a unique opportunity for children to practice mindfulness, to pause and fully engage with the place and moment they're in. By focusing on their senses during the fun, interactive moments, this deceptively simple book promotes a greater sense of belonging in children.

Kelly-Ann Allen is an Associate Professor and Educational and Developmental Psychologist at Monash University and an Honorary Principal Fellow at the Centre for Wellbeing Science at the University of Melbourne. Kelly-Ann is renowned for her impactful research on belonging, particularly in educational settings, which has earned her recognition as one of Australia's top researchers. Kelly-Ann is dedicated to translating her extensive research into practical applications to benefit educators, students, and broader communities. Her work extends beyond academia, aiming to enhance belonging across populations globally.

Michael Wagner is the Melbourne-based author of more than 90 books for children including the much-loved, 20-book Maxx Rumble series, the CBCA Honor book *Dirt by Sea* and Notable books *Why I Love Footy*, *Why I Love Summer*, and *Bear Make Den*, and the YABBA, KOALA, and KROC Awards shortlisted So Wrong series. Before becoming an author, Michael worked for ten years as a radio broadcaster with the ABC, wrote and produced award-winning animation for television, and penned everything from advertising copy to songs and comedy.

Kathryn Kallady is an Educational and Developmental Psychologist. She has worked predominantly with children and their families between the ages of 2–18 years of age. She has extensive experience working with schools in the private and public sectors as well as in public health settings. She has also worked in a private practice confident in neurodevelopmental assessment and therapy. She has worked at Monash University in a supervisory and teaching capacity. Apart from psychology, Kathryn loves illustration and graphic design. She has provided works for academic texts and resources. She is best known for providing the single artwork for Gotye's international hit song, "Somebody that I Used to Know."

Kelly

To every student who enters school in search of belonging—may you find a place where you are seen, valued, and truly loved.

To Florence, Henry, and Georgie—may your school days be filled with learning, laughter, and a lasting sense of belonging.

Michael

For Ollie-Sue who belongs right here with us, forever.

This is Ali. These are his ears.

This is Riko. These are her hands.

This is Geet. This is her nose.

This is Arthur. This is his mouth.

And this is Trixie. These are her eyes.

Ali knows he's at school when he hears:

music playing through the speakers when the day is about to begin

Mr Lee's warm welcome to the classroom

the shushes and shuffles
of kids settling in
for morning roll call

pencils clattering,
paper rustling,
and sticky tape riiiiiiipping
as everyone works

the thuds and thumps of balls bouncing in the playground and the shouting and laughter outside at lunch time.

These are the *sounds* of school for Ali. Each sound reminds him that school is a place where he belongs.

Can you think of a few sounds that are special to your school?

Riko knows she's at school when she feels:

her school bag bouncing against her back

her own hair twirling
between her fingers while
she's thinking hard

tiny balls of sticky
glue rolling between
her fingertips

her floppy hat tight on her head at lunchtime

touching the hard tanbark beneath the play equipment

and the carpet under her palm when everyone's sitting on the floor.

This is what school *feels* like to Riko. Each feeling reminds her that school is a place where she belongs.

Can you think of a few feelings that are special to your school?

Geet knows she's at school when she smells:

Miss Yindi's flowery perfume

hot food wafting from the canteen
before the lunch orders arrive

newly cut grass on the oval

a tiny pile of pencil shavings in her palm

the "lolly" smells of her special rubbers and pens

and the pages of a brand new library book.

These are the *smells* of school for Geet. And each smell reminds her that school is a place where she feels like she belongs.

Can you think of five smells that make you feel like you belong at school?

Arthur knows he's at school when he tastes:

crunchy, milky cereal at breakfast club

cut up pieces of fruit for snack time

cold, splashy water from the bubbler

a sandwich for lunch, sometimes with vegemite,
sometimes with cheese, sometimes with honey

But never all three at the same time!

sweet apple juice squirting up through a straw

and cheesy pizza on "lunch order" days.

These are the *tastes* of school for Arthur. Each one reminds him that school is a place where he belongs.

Can you think of five flavours that taste like school to you?

20

Trixie knows she's at school when she sees:

her best friend's smiling face as she's running towards her

Miss Sally's yellow dress, which is as bright as sunshine

projects hanging on the classroom wall

exciting new books on display in the library

her long lost jumper in lost property

Oh, how she missed it.

and Dad's smiling face when he comes to pick her up.

This is what school *looks* like to Trixie. When she sees each of these things, Trixie knows that school is a place where she belongs.

Can you think of five sights that make you feel like you're at school?

There are many sights, sounds, smells, tastes, and things you can feel at school. And each of them is a special reminder that…

school is where we all belong.

ABOUT THIS BOOK

Thank you for taking the time to read our book and for using it to help the children in your life develop a stronger sense of belonging.

Belonging is often described as a fundamental human need and has been found to be an essential component of wellbeing, physical health, prosocial behaviour, and academic outcomes. It can also buffer the effects of mental illness and can be a protective factor against depression and anxiety.

Belonging is largely experiential and sensory, and can be linked to certain sounds, smells, sights, textures, tastes, and sensations, which are unique and special to each person. This book encourages the reader, through the practice of mindfulness, to pause and fully engage with the place and moment they're in. By focusing on their senses during the fun, interactive moments, the reader's sense of belonging is amplified.

We all need to belong – to family, home, school, nature, the community, and the world. Our hope is that this deceptively simple book promotes a greater sense of belonging in children.